Saudi Arabia

by Laurie Halse Anderson

❧ Carolrhoda Books, Inc. / Minneapolis

Photo Acknowledgments

Photos, maps, and artwork are used courtesy of: John Erste, pp. 1, 2–3, 14–15, 21, 25, 30–31, 38–39; Middle East Pictures, pp. 4, 6, 7, 8, 9 (both), 11, 12, 13, 16, 17 (top), 20, 22 (bottom), 23 (top), 26, 27, 28, 29, 32, 36, 37 (both), 38, 39, 40, 41, 42, 43; Laura Westlund, pp. 5, 27; © TRIP/TRIP, pp. 10, 17 (bottom), 18, 19, 22 (top), 33, 34, 35; © Tor Eigeland, pp. 14, 15; © Camerapix/ Middle East Pictures, p. 21; © Wolfgang Kaehler, p. 23 (bottom); © TRIP/OP, p. 24.

Cover photo © Wolfgang Kaehler.

Carolrhoda Books, Inc.
A division of Lerner Publishing Group
241 First Avenue North
Minneapolis, Minnesota 55401 U.S.A.

Website address: www.lernerbooks.com

Words in **bold type** are explained in a glossary that begins on page 44.

Library of Congress Cataloging-in-Publication Data

Anderson, Laurie Halse.
  Saudi Arabia / Laurie Halse Anderson.
    p.   cm. — (A ticket to)
  Includes index.
  Summary: Briefly describes the people, geography, government, religion, languages, customs, and lifestyles of Saudi Arabia.
    ISBN 1–57505–147–8 (lib. bdg. : alk. paper)
    1. Saudi Arabia—Juvenile literature. [1. Saudi Arabia.] I. Title II. Series.
DS204.25.A53   2001   00–009275
965—dc21

Manufactured in the United States of America
1 2 3 4 5 6 – JR – 06 05 04 03 02 01

Contents

Welcome!

Saudi Arabia covers most of the **Arabian Peninsula.** The country is in the **Middle East,** part of the **continent** of Asia. The Red Sea is west of Saudi Arabia. In the east are Qatar, Kuwait, the United Arab Emirates, and the Persian Gulf. Iraq and Jordan sit to the north. Southward lie Oman and Yemen.

Desert landscapes greet Saudi Arabia's visitors.

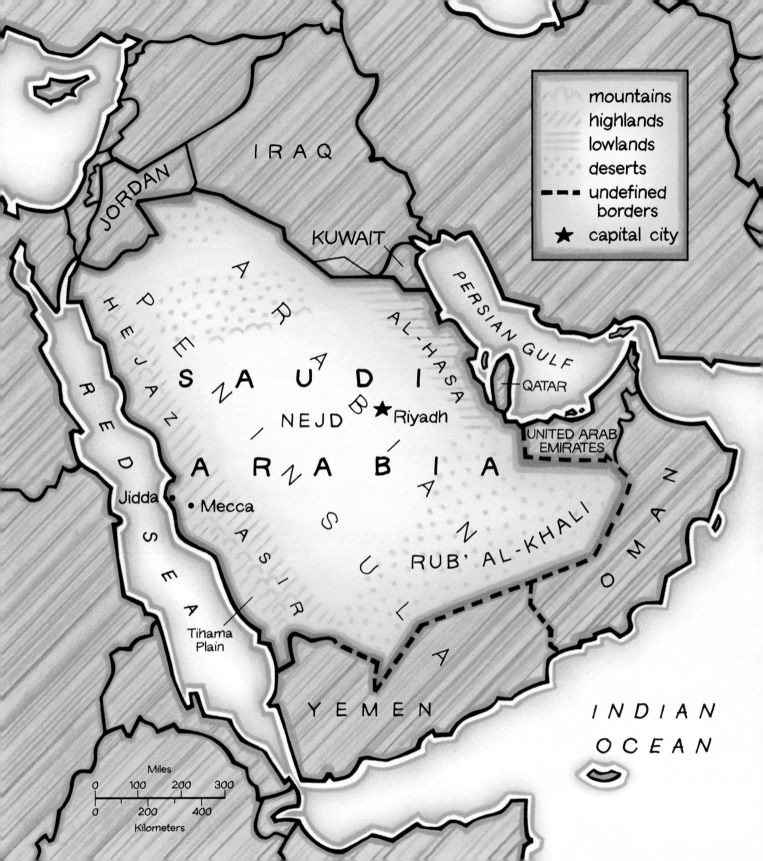

IRAQ

JORDAN

KUWAIT

PERSIAN GULF

AL-HASA

QATAR

UNITED ARAB
EMIRATES

A
R
A
B
I
A
N

P
E
N
I
N
S
U
L
A

SAUDI

NEJD ★ Riyadh

ARABIA

H
E
J
A
Z

A
S
I
R

RED SEA

Jidda • Mecca

Tihama
Plain

RUB' AL-KHALI

OMAN

YEMEN

INDIAN
OCEAN

mountains
highlands
lowlands
deserts
- - - undefined
borders
★ capital city

Miles
0   100   200   300

0   200   400
Kilometers

Across the Country

Much of Saudi Arabia is **desert,** but not all of it. The Hejaz region runs along the Red Sea's coast. Beaches and cliffs rise to hills and mountains. South of Hejaz, farms blanket the Tihama **Plain.** In the **mountains** of the Asir region, farmers raise fruit trees.

A huge rocky **plateau** region called the Nejd stretches eastward. Lush, green **oases** dot the Nejd, where most Saudis live. North of the Nejd, a desert meets Jordan and Iraq.

A hiker pauses at the edge of a dry Hejaz canyon (facing page).

Map Whiz Quiz

Check the map on page 5! Trace the map onto a piece of paper. Can you find the Red Sea? Color it red and mark it with a "W" for west. Now find the Persian Gulf. Color it blue and mark it with an "E" for east.

The Asir Mountains have lush farmland (right).

7

Sandy deserts stretch over miles of Saudi Arabia.

Deserts and Oil

Salt flats and gravel plains border the Persian Gulf. About a quarter of the world's supply of oil lies beneath this region called Al-Hasa.

A desert called Rub' al-Khali (the Empty Quarter) covers southeastern Saudi Arabia. Rub' al-Khali is the driest, hottest place on earth. In the summer, temperatures of 120 degrees can make thermometers explode!

Pipes and valves mark the site of an oil well (above). A sandstorm (left) can last for days. The blowing sand can damage buildings and trees.

Family Life

Saudi families are
very close. Kids live
near aunts, uncles,
cousins, and
grandparents. The
family gets together
about once a week.

*A proud Saudi dad brings his kids
to the park to play.*

According to
tradition, men go
to work, take care of the shopping, and run
errands. Women raise children and run the
house. In modern times, some women find
jobs outside the home.

All in the Family

Here are the Arabic names for family members.
Try them out on your own family!

grandfather	*jeddee*	(ZHED-ee)
grandmother	*jeddatee*	(ZHED-ah-tee)
father	*eb*	(EHB)
mother	*omun*	(OH-moon)
uncle	*omi*	(AAHM-ee)
aunt	*omti*	(AAHM-tee)
brother	*okh*	(OAK)
sister	*okht*	(OH-kit)
son	*wuld*	(WILD)
daughter	*bent*	(BINT)

Saudis and tourists stroll through a shopping district.

The Saudis

About 20 million people make their homes in Saudi Arabia. Most Saudis are **Arabs.** Saudi families are grouped into **tribes.** Their families have lived on the Arabian Peninsula for thousands of years. Each tribe

Abdul Aziz Ibn Sa'ud

In 1932 Abdul Aziz Ibn Sa'ud became the first king of Saudi Arabia. He was a generous leader and a devout **Muslim.** He worked with Islamic leaders to decide what parts of modern-day lifestyles should be allowed in Saudi Arabia.

defended an area of the country. In modern times, 80 tribes live in Saudi Arabia. Most Saudis are very proud of their tribe.

A man from the Tihama Plain wears the traditional clothing of his tribe.

Desert Nomads

About 10 percent of Saudis are **nomads.** Saudi nomads herd goats and sheep. They move from place to place and camp in tents. Most modern-day Saudi nomads stay near schools and hospitals.

Nomads prepare to dig into dinner. Would you like to join them? A Saudi host would welcome you to the meal.

In the past, many Saudis lived as nomads. Saudi culture comes from desert traditions.

A nomad herder watches over his animals.

One desert tradition is generosity to guests. No one can live alone in the desert, so nomads treat their guests like family.

15

Many Saudi Arabian buildings are white. The light color helps buildings stay cool in the hot sun.

City Saudis

About 70 percent of Saudi Arabians live in cities. Saudi Arabia's modern cities boast schools, hospitals, roads, malls, airports, grocery stores, parks, and soccer stadiums! Gardens with fountains and pools of water dot the cities.

City dwellers live in houses or apartments with two living rooms. One is for men and one is for women.

Many Saudi buildings have central courtyards with cool fountains.

Rugs and pillows cover the floor of this Saudi home.

17

Religion

Islam is the religion of Saudi Arabia. Islam is the basis for Saudi daily life, law, government, schools, and much more. All Saudi Arabians and most guest workers are Muslims (followers of Islam).

Muslims believe in one God, Allah. Muslims believe that the prophet Muhammad received Allah's messages.

A Muslim woman takes time out of her day to pray.

Many Muslims prize old decorated Korans.

The messages became the Koran, the holy book of Islam. Kids celebrate the first time that they read the Koran.

A Holy Time

Ramadan, the holiest month to Muslims, is a time of **fasting.** Muslims can't eat or drink from sunup to sundown during Ramadan. After dark they pray at a **mosque,** then eat a big meal.

Times to Pray

Muslims pray at dawn, noon, midafternoon, sunset, and nightfall—five times each day. Business stops at prayer time. Before praying, Muslims wash themselves. Muslims face Mecca, the holiest city of Islam, when they pray. Mecca is in western Saudi Arabia.

Mosques (Muslim places of worship) have tall towers. Five times a day, a call to prayer is broadcast from the top of the tower.

Muslims have five main beliefs called the Pillars of Islam (below). The beliefs are sawm (*going without food at certain times*), zakat (*giving to charity*), hajj (*a religious journey*), salaat (*prayer five times a day*) and shahada (*belief in God*).

Muslims from all over the world pray at the Great Mosque in Mecca (above).

sawm

zakat

hajj

salaat

shahada

Cover Up!

Most Saudis wear traditional clothing. Men wear a white shirt, called a *thobe*, that goes all the way to the ground.

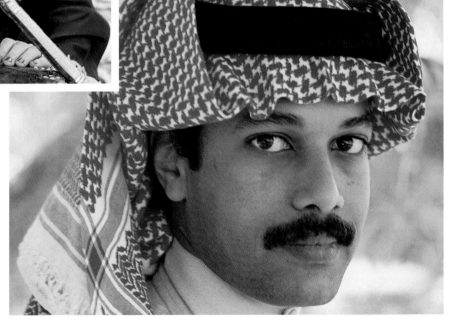

Women's headgear traditionally covers their hair and faces (above). This man has chosen a red and white checked cloth (right).

A large piece of cloth, held on by a black cord, protects a man's head.

Many women pick beautiful, brightly colored outfits.

Women go shopping in their abbayahs.

But in public, they cover up with a black, robelike *abbayah.*

This Saudi boy wears a thobe.

23

Saudi boys play soccer in the courtyard of a home.

Kid Life

The **extended family's** love surrounds a Saudi child. Families help kids decide what to study at school, what kind of job to have, and who to marry. Kids respect their older relatives and follow their advice.

Popular Pets

The cat is the number-one pet in Saudi Arabia. Other popular pets include rabbits and birds. You will not find a dog in anyone's home. They are not considered clean enough to come indoors. Dogs are farm animals and live outside, where they can guard sheep.

Merchants and customers haggle over prices at a fish souk.

Souk Shopping

A souk, or marketplace, is one of the most exciting places in a Saudi Arabian city or town. If you visit, you will hear chickens clucking and merchants laughing. The air smells of spices, coffee, and incense. Fires crackle under grilling lamb. Gold jewelry flashes in the sun.

City dwellers can visit a modern, air-conditioned shopping mall. The mall's stores sell clothes and goods.

Dear Pete,

Saudi Arabia is awesome! In Jidda we spent hours in the souk. Dad bought a hand-woven rug. He bargained with the seller until they agreed on a low price. We snacked on roast lamb. Then we went for a drive in the desert. It looks like it goes on forever!

Love,
Yousif

A jeweler shows his wares to a pair of mall shoppers.

Arabic ABCs

A Saudi businessman jots down some notes.

The language of Saudi Arabia is Arabic. Writers in Arabic don't use the same alphabet as writers in English do.

People write Arabic from right to left. Readers turn book pages from left to right. That's the opposite way that people read books written in English. But to Saudi Arabians, English-language books look backwards!

The Saudi Arabian Flag

The Saudi Arabian flag shows Arabic words and a sword. The words read, "There is no God but Allah, and Muhammad is his prophet." The sword shows that Saudis will fight to spread Islam.

Poems and Stories

Saudis love poetry! They chant it, write it, and read it. Many Saudis enjoy poems about brave people and daring deeds. Some Saudis enjoy **folktales** about animals. Stories of magic and wild adventures are popular, too.

Who Lied?

According to a folktale, some nomads were once looking for new grazing land for sheep. The nomads sent the crow, the partridge, and the dove to search. The crow returned. He said that he found only desert and no grass. The other two birds returned and said that they had discovered lots of grass. The tribe followed the partridge and the dove and found what they said was true. Because the crow had lied, they painted him black. The nomads rewarded the partridge by lining her eyes with kohl (a dark eye makeup) and the dove by painting her feet pink.

Time for School

Schoolboys work on art projects as their teacher looks on.

In Saudi Arabia, classes start at six in the morning. The school day begins early so that classes can end before it gets very hot outside. School ends at about one in the afternoon.

Saudi boys and girls study in separate schools. They study math, Arabic, history, science, and Islam.

Girls listen to tapes and watch a film in a language class.

Are you hungry? A Saudi meal might include a relish tray, a salad, bread, and eggplant dip.

Big Lunch!

Lunch is the biggest meal of the day. Saudis gather at home for lunch. They might eat lettuce, cucumbers, tomatoes, rice, and lamb stew. A family living by the Persian Gulf might choose freshly caught fish. After lunch many people rest for a few hours. It is too hot to do much else! Children who don't want to nap might read or do homework.

Coffee Break

Serving tiny cups of coffee is a Saudi tradition. The host serves the oldest or most important person first. Saudis consider it polite to drink two cupfuls but not three! To refuse the third serving of coffee, a Saudi waggles the cup back and forth.

Carry Your Art

Saudi Arabia is famous for its fancy carpets.

It is hard to find a place for fancy art in a tent. So nomadic Saudis created beautiful everyday objects, such as carpets and fancy saddles for camels and horses. Saudis treasure these objects in modern times, too.

Many Saudis admire beautiful jewelry. Some Saudis wear five bracelets or rings.

This man holds a
fancy incense
burner (above).

Five is considered a lucky number. Children like to wear bell-trimmed anklets and bracelets.

Fountains decorate some public spaces. This fountain (below) is shaped like a treasure chest.

Sword Dance

The national dance of Saudi Arabia is the sword dance, called the *ardha.* Men stand shoulder to shoulder in rows and face the same direction.

A Saudi man plays a traditional instrument.

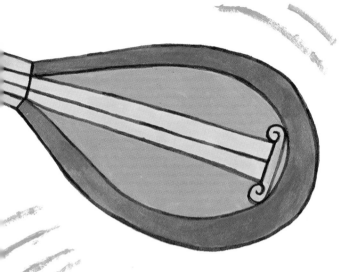

In the center of the group, a poet sings while drummers beat a rhythm. The men step and sway, waving their swords in the air and moving forward. The dance can be done with just a few people or with hundreds.

Saudi men hold their swords high during the ardha.

Fireworks mark the end of Ramadan.

Celebrate!

A three-day festival marks the end of **Ramadan.** Families attend prayers in the mosque, then go home to exchange gifts

The Great Camel Race begins the Janadriyah Heritage Festival.

and enjoy a feast. Many people wear new clothes and give gifts to the poor.

Each March Saudis celebrate their culture with the Janadriyah Heritage Festival. Poets recite famous verses, people display their crafts, and dancers perform.

Fun in Saudi Arabia

Falconry is a traditional Saudi sport. Saudis admire falconry in modern times. Falcons are fierce birds of prey.

Saudi men gather for a day of falconing.

People train falcons to catch other birds. Falcon trainers treat their birds with care.

Many Saudi families like camping in the desert. They bring a tent, a picnic, and plenty of water. Campers nap during the hottest part of the day. They stay awake long into the cooler night.

A family enjoys a Friday evening picnic in the desert. Does your family do something special each week?

New Words to Learn

Arab: A person who speaks Arabic, belonging to the ethnic group from the Arabian Peninsula.

Arabian Peninsula: A peninsula in southwestern Asia bordered by the Red Sea, the Arabian Sea, and the Gulf of Aden (all of which belong to the Indian Ocean).

continent: Any of the seven large areas of land. The continents are Africa, Antarctica, Asia, Australia, Europe, North America, and South America.

desert: A dry, sandy region that receives low amounts of rainfall.

extended family: Mothers, fathers, brothers, sisters, grandparents, aunts, uncles, and cousins who often live together in one household.

fasting: Going without eating or drinking.

folktales: Traditional stories told for generations.

Middle East: The countries of North Africa and southwestern Asia from Libya in the west to Afghanistan in the east.

mosque: Muslim place of worship.

mountain: Part of the earth's surface that rises into the sky.

Muslim: A follower of the religion Islam.

nomad: A person who moves from place to place, following seasonal sources of water and food.

oases: Places that have water and vegetation in the middle of the desert.

plain: A broad, flat area of land that has few trees or other outstanding natural features.

plateau: A region of level land that is above most of the surrounding territory.

Ramadan: The ninth month of the Islamic year, and the holiest time of the year for Muslims. During Ramadan, Muslims fast from dawn to sunset.

tradition: A way of doing things—such as preparing a meal, celebrating a holiday, or making a living—that a group of people practice.

tribe: A group of families who have a common ancestor.

New Words to Say

Al-Hasa	ahl-ah-HAH-suh
Asir	a-SIHR
Hejaz	heh-JAZ
Janadriyah	jah-nah-DREE-yah
Jidda	JIHD-dah
Koran	koh-RAHN
Mecca	MEHK-kah
Nejd	NAHJD
Ramadan	RAH-mah-dahn
Riyadh	REE-yad
souk	SOOK
Tihama	tee-HAH-muh

More Books to Read

Al Hoad, Abdul Latif. *We Live in Saudi Arabia.* New York: The Bookwright Press, 1987.

Dutton, Roderic. *An Arab Family.* Minneapolis: Lerner Publications Company, 1980.

Foster, Leila Merrell. *Saudi Arabia: Enchantment of the World.* Chicago: Childrens Press, 1993.

Haskins, Jim. *Count Your Way Through the Arab World.* Minneapolis: Carolrhoda Books, 1987.

Williams, Marcia. *Sinbad the Sailor.* Cambridge, MA: Candlewick Press, 1994.

New Words to Find